Colin's Courage

Creator and illustrator: Patrick Arguin

English translation: Bleu Dactylo

French version written by: Michèle Rappe
Support, coaching and collaboration: Hélène Beaudette

I want to offer my deepest gratitude to Hélène Beaudette.
Her unconditional support and presence allowed TOOLS OF THE HEART to grow and come into form.

The summer is slowly ending.
Colin is taking a nap and enjoying the warm
and soothing rays of Father Sun. His friend
Fluffy has gone to explore the river banks.

Grubber, the raccoon, is searching the
garden for food when he notices some acorns
at Colin's foot.

«Oh goody goody!» And without hesitating,
he gobbles the acorns up.

Colin suddenly wakes up and notices Grubber finishing his meal and licking his fingers. The oak knows how rude Grubber can be, but he is not bitter and still greets him.

«Hello there Grubber, did you eat well?»

«Nope!» replies Grubber. «Your acorns are too small, and they taste awful!» Then he runs away laughing.

Colin feels sadness rising within him.
«My acorns taste bad,» he thinks,
«and Grubber is right, they are too small!»

All day long, the oak's worry keeps on growing.
He wonders why Grubber did not like his acorns.
How can his acorns taste better?

Colin cannot stop thinking about what the raccoon said, and he feels very sad.

He then decides to go into his heart to find his rainbow of wisdom. He knows that this will help him to find his peace again.

After long and deep breaths, Colin starts to relax, and he is not surprised to see an elf wearing one of the colors of the rainbow: Indigo.

The elf addresses Colin:
«Dear Colin, throughout your life as an oak, there will always be someone to criticize or mock you.»

Colin feels Indigo's kindness and listens to him.

«It may happen that some people will say lies about you or try to make fun of you. Always remember this: what is important is what YOU think about yourself!»

Colin understands but at the same time, it's easier said than done!

«Think about the pleasure Fluffy has when he is enjoying your acorns; think about all the beautiful qualities you have and the wonderful oak tree that you have become,» says Indigo.

Colin feels a soft indigo light hugging him with love, and something special growing in his heart.

«What you are feeling,» explains Indigo, «is your self-worth. It is inside your heart at all times; you can always find it and listen to it.»

«You have the choice to believe others or not and you have the choice to let it bother you or not.»

Colin opens his eyes and feels good again. He remembers Indigo's words and realizes how quickly he believed Grubber's lies.

Fluffy returns from the river and joins his happy friend. How sweet it is to be together!

At Colin's foot, Grubber and his raccoon friends are searching for food. They are also making fun of Colin.

«Give us acorns!» he demands rudely.

«You are not nice to me,» says Colin, «and I choose not to give you any acorns! Since you think they taste awful, I will keep them for my friends who appreciate them.»

The raccoons are very surprised!

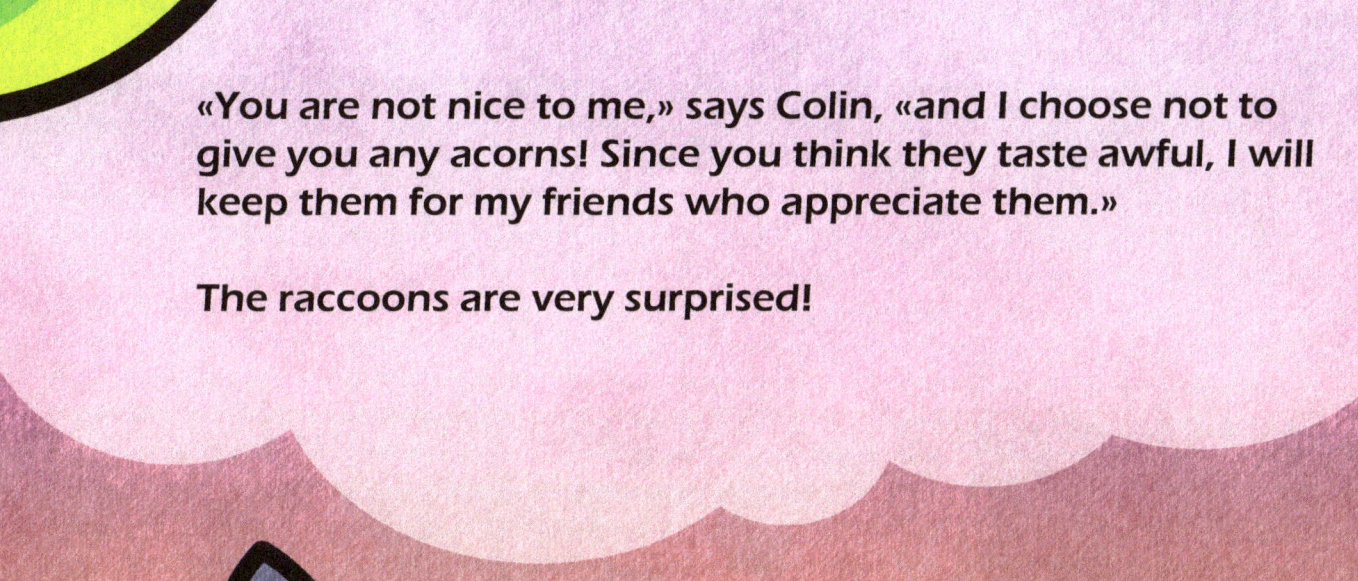

The band of raccoons left with empty stomachs. Fluffy looks up to his friend thinking how courageous he was. Colin is proud of him. He knows his acorns taste good, even if some people do not appreciate them!

Fluffy finishes his last acorn before going to sleep.
The night is softly settling in, and Colin notices that
it is almost the same color as the Indigo elf.

Remember...

Why do we sometimes get criticized?

Everyone has different tastes and needs. Some people do not always like what is different from them. They either fear it or don't understand it, and so they criticize it. That is why it is important to know your own value and remain confident in yourself!

What can I do if what I hear makes me sad?

If you feel sad, take the time to go into your heart and remember your qualities, which truly are worth a thousand treasures! If it's possible, tell those who criticized you that you did not like it and explain why.

What if it continues?

You can choose to end a relationship if you do not feel well or respected anymore. Stay courageous and kindly explain your choice. You can also seek help from a grown-up who will guide you in expressing your feelings.

The Book Collection

Tools of the Heart
Fostering Confidence and Self-esteem

1 **Father Sun and Mother Earth Create Life**
Breathing/Finding your rhythm
Breathing is essential to life; conscious breathing is a simple, yet effective way to regain your calm and well-being by finding your body's rhythm.

2 **Fluffy and the Rainbow in his Heart**
Meditation/Finding your inner calm
Each one of us has a peaceful place inside their heart. Meditation is a tool that allows you to find your personal space or to go back to it.

3 **Colin Discovers Confidence**
Grounding/Strengthening your self-confidence
Growing up often comes with its share of fears and hesitations. Growing solid roots helps to build and nurture a positive self-confidence.

4 **Colin and Fluffy Become Friends**
Knowing yourself/Loving and appreciating
Positive self-confidence and self-esteem are the building blocks of healthy relationships; therefore, learning to appreciate who we are is a treasure for life.

5 **The Choice**
Insight/Listening to your intuition
Learning to listen to your inner voice and how to trust it, is learning to stay true to yourself in all situations.

6 **Colin's Courage**
Expressing/Confidence in yourself
Standing up for yourself is not wrong. It is about relying on your self-worth with confidence, to respectfully say what you need to say.

7 **Enough is Enough**
Self-respect/Daring to be yourself
Developing good communication skills also implies expressing your feelings and needs in a respectful manner, which can sometimes be a challenge!

8 **Fluffy Finds his Well-being**
Self-awareness/Taking responsibility
Growing up is also about becoming more aware of your emotions and learning to manage them responsibly.

The Meditation Collection

Tools of the Heart
Fostering Confidence and Self-esteem

Specially designed for young children, the guided meditations explore and develop the same themes, as seen in the **Tools of the Heart** book collection. These intend to reinforce the children's knowledge of themselves through their inner space of wisdom, where things can be seen, heard, and felt.

Meditation is also a wonderful tool that children can easily learn to help them self-regulate physically, mentally, and emotionally.

To learn more, go to our website:
www.toolsoftheheart.com